Spike's Holiday Book
James R. Bower

Halloween

Thanksgiving

Christmas

Copyright © 2019 James R. Bowker

All rights reserved. No part of this book may be reproduced or transmitted in any form or by any means, electronic or mechanical, including photocopying, recording or by any information storage and retrieval system, without permission in writing from the publisher.

Average Dog Publishing– Deer Park, TX
ISBN: 978-1-7337590-4-5
Library of Congress Card Control Number: 2019917921
My Silly Dog Spike | James R. Bower
Available Formats: | Paperback distribution

About the Author

James R. Bower, retired designer of architectural and mechanical engineering, a U.S. Paratrooper Veteran of the 60's and 70's. I now spend my time getting back to my artwork pencil drawing and painting. I used to raise horses, cattle and buffalo on my ranch in Texas but retired from that also. I was born and raised in Michigan, I moved to Texas in 1981. I'm married with 5 kids, 12 grand kids and 4 great grand kids.

"Hey fella's Halloween is getting very close, said Socks. Yippee! that's right," said Boss.

"We better get planning on our costumes and party," said Spike.

"Hey fella's Halloween is getting very close, said Socks.Yippee! that's right," said Boss.

"We better get planning on our costumes and party," said Spike.

"Let's go find us a big pumpkin," said Spike.
"Let's go," said Boss and Socks.
So, off the boys went in search of a big pumpkin.

The boys are headed back home with their pumpkin.

The boys get ready to carve their pumpkin.
"I'll draw the face," said Boss.
"I'll do the cleaning and cut out the face," said Spike.
"I'll go find a candle," said Socks.

"The boys are finished carving their pumpkin. Look how it glows," said Socks.
Spike is admiring his carving work while Boss is getting excited about going Trick or Treating this evening.

It's finally time to go Trick or Treating and Boss has been waiting all day for this. By being so small he has to wait for Spike and Socks before he could go.

The boy's bags are full of candy bars, suckers, tootsie rolls, bubble gum and popcorn balls. Oh boy, I can't wait to get home and eat my candy, said Boss. We still have our party to go to, says Spike and Socks.

With their bags full of candy, the boys head home to get ready for the party. Also, so Boss could eat some of his candy.

"You did it Spike," said Socks.
"Bobbing for apples looks like fun," said Boss. The boys are having lots of fun at the Halloween party.

As time went on by, it soon was time for Thanksgiving and the boys wanted to celebrate it like the first Thanksgiving, the way the Pilgrims did.

Spike, Boss and Socks are coming ashore on the new land, just as the Pilgrims did.

Spike is making new friends with the Native people of the new land, just as the Pilgrims did when they first arrived.

Let's make camp here, Spike says. Looks great to us, said Boss and Socks. So, the boys started setting up their camp site.

Socks and Boss are collecting wood for their campfire, while Spike is out looking around the area.

Boss says, I'll build the campfire. Mean while Socks is gathering more firewood and Spike is looking for a Turkey.

I'll go find us a Turkey, said Spike..

The Native Americans brought Squash, Corn, Turkey and more to share with the new Pilgrims that have arrived.

A big feast is ready for the re-enactment of the first Thanksgiving.

This is great, said Boss. Yes, now we have Thanksgiving said, Socks. We also made new friends with the Native Indians at the same time, said Spike.

Another month went by and Christmas was soon upon us.

It won't be long before Christmas, said Boss. That's right, said Socks. You fella's are trying to make time go by too fast, said Spike.

The Boys have gone to town to do some Christmas Shopping.

It's time for the Christmas play. Spike, Boss and Socks are playing the three Wisemen.

Let's decorate the tree as soon as we get home, said Boss. That would be fun, said Socks. We will see what time it is when we get home, said Spike.

The boys got the tree home and started to decorate it. Boss got his wish!

The boys decided to go out and sing some Christmas Carols after they decorated their Christmas tree.

Wow! This is fun, said Boss. It sure is, hang on to your hat Boss, said Socks. This is a great hill to slide down, said Spike.

The boys are listening to the little one's Christmas wishes.

Christmas morning arrived and the boys got to open their gifts. Spike, Boss, and Socks are wishing everyone a very Happy New Year.

Socks

Spike

Boss

www.ingramcontent.com/pod-product-compliance
Lightning Source LLC
Chambersburg PA
CBHW061226070526
44584CB00029B/4007